CALL MY NAME

Heather Wyatt

A Publication of The Poetry Box©

Editing & Book Design by Shawn Aveningo Sanders
Cover Design by Robert R. Sanders

ISBN: 978-1-948461-28-3
Printed in the United States of America.

Published by The Poetry Box©, 2019
Beaverton, Oregon
ThePoetryBox.com

For Allie

CONTENTS

Call My Name

– 1 –

Startled,
you place your hand
above your brow,
squint your tired eyes
and tell me to watch out
for the children running
toward us. I don't have the heart
to tell you it is Dorothy
and her yellow brick road
that you were seeing instead.

– 2 –

This is not the first
or last poem I will write
about you.
This time I am trying
to decide what I want
from your house
that you can't fit
in your tiny room.
How can I choose
what I want
to take with me?

We haven't even had
a funeral for you.

– 3 –

Out of the thousands
of rocking horses you have,

I want the one
made from hand-blown
crystal that says
1982 World's Fair,
the hundreds of clip-on
pearls you wore
because you never
pierced your ears,
the ceramic, hand painted
water pipe you bought
from Turkey in the sixties
when you didn't know
what it was,
your copies of *Ragtime* and *Scarlett,*
the quilt you made
that kept you warm
on the couch you had
for forty years,
and the World's Greatest Aunt
magnet I gave you.

– 4 –

You had an elastic pride
like no one I ever knew.
Now, you scream for Viola,
Brenda, Winnie, and
none of them are me.
The closet is your refrigerator
and you are on the kitchen floor
and you are in the fabrics department
and you are working.
You fold the same stiff, sterile sheet
for hours and look desperately
at the oxygen machine to give
you a price for the discounted fabric.
The wail that comes from you all night

is perverse like a screeching, dying animal
and you tug at your IV
repeatedly until the nurses insist
you be restrained.
You call for a customer's attention
and when I tell you to get some sleep,
you bunch the fabric of my shirt on my chest
and pull me close to your face
and tell me that you will hit me
if I don't get you out.

– 5 –

Now, you sit
in a nursing home
and your neighbor
sits in silence
slumped over,
like an empty duffle bag
and you stare out
the window and cry.
I want you to know
that my name is not
Viola or Brenda.

I want you to be right
when you say
you aren't like the other
women in the home.

I want you to be moving
back to your apartment,
ever.

I want you to call me Heather

Nostalgic Scroll

dense fog seeping up from the ground at school
broken pieces of red crayons strewn around my nap mat
grime on the penny I threw to a homeless man on the streets
      of Miami at age five
my second grade class on the playground from afar
      when the teacher told them I had lice
chunks of ground round bubbling around powdered
      cheese and elbow macaroni
miniature teapot I begged my mother for after Aunt
      Francis died
yellow crocheted purse from Great-Grandmother Maude
fallen hair from Barbie on Salon day
sand dunes perched on the coast of North Carolina
      littered with kites donning images of
      superheroes
sixteenth century forts, lighthouses bigger than life
      and miles of white beaches in St. Augustine
state magnets from truck stops and their geographical
      position on the refrigerator
tears and smudged cigarette ashes on the ground
      below my grandmother when we moved away
seas of crimson, white and turf green on Saturdays
clumps of marijuana stuffed in the center of coke
      cans on the way to school
plump thighs and cheeks in my mirror
grabbing the leash from the nook in the laundry room
      to walk my dog

Misbehaving

Grandma's attic was
a place to find treasures,
her spare cigarettes,
Dad's hidden 8-tracks.

The heat in the summer
made drops of sweat
rush from my nape
down my back.

It was
almost
unbearable.

The stairs stored
Cokes and Christmas
toys and my Grandpa's
leather golf bag.

I ran my fingers
down the driver
and crept outside
with it in my hand.

I went to the edge
of the garden
and with my heart
ascending to my throat
I plucked red apples
from the tree,
placed them snugly
in the grass,
swung, with eyes tight shut
as hard as I could

waiting for them to thud.

I could hear
the screen
door open
but I didn't care,
I just kept going,
swing, after swing.

Dig

We dug
with an urgent
fury. If we were
going to make it
to China by dinner
we had no time to stop.

The empty juice boxes
were stacked beside
our dirt piles
and we were both armed
with garden shovels
digging different holes,
our fingers
grimy with red mud.

I told you I had to use
the bathroom.
You pointed to the driveway
behind the white,
plastic chairs
and Fisher Price toys.
There was no time
for bathroom breaks.

I ran, squatted down
over the rocky driveway
and pulled down
my pedal pushers.
I couldn't believe
the relief.
My eyes followed
the warm stream
all the way down

the pebbled drive.

Running in horror,
my friend came
to warn me as my
mother's car pulled up.

She saw what we were doing.
Fire in my cheeks,
I hopped up
and eased my
elastic pants back
to my belly button.

My mother said nothing
storming in my direction,
tripping in one of our holes.

The Price is Right

Every time I smell
canned ravioli,
I think of Bob Barker
and *The Price is Right*.

I watched in Grandma's
den every day,
sometimes eating ravioli
from the lunch pail,
sometimes eating
Vienna sausage.

Grandpa would
pluck the strings
on his guitar
until he heard
creaking floor boards
that meant Grandma
was coming to tell
him to stop.

I spent every
summer this way,
reclining, looking
at the wood paneling
on the walls.

I still flip
the TV channels,
looking for Plinko,
searching for the smell
of Chef Boyardee.

Great Grandmother Maude's Funeral

You made hot dogs and tater tots
when I knew you but my father
told us stories of roast and potatoes
from your younger days.

I had surgery that Christmas
on my foot, about a week
before you died at age 96.
The steel crutches
provided little support
for my heavy cast.

At your funeral,
I hopped up the ramp,
and with one mindless
motion, the rubber end
of the crutch slipped
on the yellow paint
and I landed, hard
on the pavement.

Dad laughed.
Mom rushed to help,
scowling at him,
while my ego bruised
like my body would later.
I lay sprawled across the entry
of the home.

Regaining composure,
I stood up, took two
hops, lost control

and my body heaved
towards the ground,
crutches flying.

I laid there
longer this time,
searched everywhere
for my dignity.
The funeral director
took control
of the crutches
showing me how
I was using them wrong.

I made it in to see you,
finally, and I wished
your cheeks were
rosy,
like
mine.

Wedding in Cumberland County, Tennessee

My uncle's toothpick
hung from his mouth
as he walked my cousin
Marie down the aisle.

His chest hair peeked
above his leather vest
and his round belt buckle
shone bright above his
black Wrangler jeans.

Aunt Freddie,
a padded box
in baby pink
was the hostess
on the mountain
that day.

Under the tent
at the reception
I let the white
bread and pimento
cheese rest in my
cheeks before
swallowing.

I stood in front
of the box fan
and watched
as my Grandma
shook hands.

Her Mouth

My brother
has a hickey.

I should have known
when the only noise

I heard was cartoons
from his room

that the trashy
leech-lipped girl

was destroying the sanctity
of my brother's neck.

When they came
out of his room

I eased my foot out
and tripped her

to the ground.
I shrugged as she turned

apple-red and glared at me.
"Oh, be careful dear."

Smoke Break

Outside today
smoking a cigarette,
I notice the neighbors'
bright red berries
on the holly bush
looking quite lovely
against his white porch.

Through the haze
of filtered tar
I see that my holly bush
has no berries
to compliment the vintage
brick of my apartment.

This young neighbor of mine
has peed in the bush,
broken beer bottles above it
backed his car into it
and still
those bright, plump berries
emerge while my dismal
holly sticks me
as I walk by
and its crunchy brown leaves
crowd my driveway.

I flick my cigarette
right in the center of it—
dreaming of it caught
in flames.

After My Second Hurricane

It was hard to see the beauty
of the Spanish-French architecture.
The streets of New Orleans smell
like old trash filled
with aged, Creole spices
and for the third time,
my blister-ridden foot
has splashed
into a urine-soaked puddle.
Purple and gold beads
were flying at my head.

I ask the homeless man
humming to himself which way
I should go and he said I
was gorgeous and beautiful—
hopped up and did a dance.

I gave him a dollar
and he gave me directions.

Hung-Over

Every time he hits the drum
my brain and skull
crackle from the pressure,
heavy on my ears.
I am trying with all my mind
to reach that note,
high, like a boiling teapot.
I should feel guilty
but I am angry at God
for this ill-deserved
punishment. I'm still
wearing my bar funk
and bad attitude
at church this morning,
like many before,
but this time I made
no promise to stop
drinking on Saturday nights.
Instead, I promised to stop
going to church
on Sunday mornings.

Vindication

I stare upward
after you make
a surprisingly loud
thud in my light fixture.
You and your kind
have invaded my house.
Swarms of thousands,
red, with black dots,
a design to imply innocence
but you fly at my mouth
and eyes.
So, I see you, bouncing
in the burning fixture
heading close to the bulb
and I watch, wishing
I had popcorn.

File Footage

I saw my ass on the news last night.
The anchor spoke of a binge eating
epidemic and then the clip appeared.
Cocking my head to the side
and making my eyes focus,
I finally recognized the familiar shape.

Almost like a heart, it bobbled,
a teeter totter unaware of the camera.
This isn't good. I said this to myself.
I put down the cookie dough.
I predicted this would happen one day.

At work today, I walk crablike,
back straight up from side to side.
No one has asked my ass
how it feels to be famous
and I hope no one ever will.

Exercising Again

Jagged pieces of wood
wedge into my shins,
deeper with each step.

Inhaling is
tiny needles
scraping my chest
and ribcage.

The hill is steeper
than I thought
and with each step
I think about letting myself
tumble down.

Even though
my back
is sweaty
and throbbing

I walk—
not crawl
into the house
and get in a cold shower

and swear
I'll walk
again
tomorrow.

Most Nights

Most nights we stare at the popcorn ceiling
instead of the stars,
listen to the sounds of the television
rather than the summer cicada.
I don't run to you in slow motion
while the waves crash on the beach
but my head rests perfectly in the hairy nook
between your chest and arm.
We have never visited Paris
but clink icy mugs
together
while we play darts.
We leave crumbs in our bed
and have to contort our bodies
to have room for the dog.
I look up at you and your crow's
feet dance as you smile
and that's the only cliché that we need.

Full of Grace

Made of stone,
she stands prim,
high, cream
stone against
the brick wall,
nailed
to a black
L bracket
looking over
the leather,
teal sofas
and the television
that never
stops running
the news ticker.
Only a small
percentage
that pass her
now cross
their hearts
as they walk
by. No golden
rosaries to view.
No reverence
in Her honor.
She looks plastic,
worn, ignored
and deeply sad.
I notice this today
and though she
is a statue, a mere
symbol meant
for décor
I cross
my heart before her.

A Caged Bird

Black eyes shift to the right—
The yellow feather erect
on top of your head.
A red cheek patch prominent on your face.
Sick, you sit in the bottom
of your cage, puffing your feathers
when you feel cold.
Your curled beak and nails
grasp at the wires—
you squawk when you can
catch your breath.
The latch that keeps you caged
comes unhinged and the door opens.

You don't leave.

Walk

I take a walk
with my dog
on a familiar path
behind a school
near my home.
We are going faster
than I would like
as my Labrador mix
with a tiny head
races for nothing.

There are still patches
of green because the winter
is mild.
I don't wear a jacket.

The street seems old,
with imperfections
and the trees ignore
us on our path.

My dog stops
to lift his leg
and the thought
crosses my mind
that this is far less poetic
than stopping by woods
on a snowy evening
or not stopping for death
before it kindly stops for me.

I cross the road
and as usual
the dog pauses

on the yellow lines,
waiting for me
to tug his leash
or tell a silly joke.

Slipping behind a fence,
I walk and slide
over the acorns
and go around
the corner of the school.
Down the hill,
I see a funnel ball game
that wobbles
at the top.
I used to play
with my own rules
counting more points
when the ball
fell through
my favorite color.
The edges are rusty
and the primary colors
are faded
but it still has purpose.

I look at the baseball
fields and hills,
familiar and fantastic.

Trudging along,
there are giant tires
ridden with red mud.
They seem misplaced—
stacked up there
in the middle
surrounded by scrap wood.

Coming back, I stroll
past the same indignant trees
I stop to look at their leaves—
scattered, purple onion peels.

This time,
I wave at the trees
and give them
no chance to ignore me.

Acknowledgments

I would like to thank the following journals for publishing these poems, in some cases in a slightly different format:

"Vindication" published in *Public Republic* (2009)

"Wedding in Cumberland County, Tennessee" published *in Broad River Review* (2011)

"Call My Name" published in *Blinking Cursor Literary Magazine*, Issue 7 (Autumn 2011) and reprinted in *The Burden of Light: Poems of Illness and Loss* (2014)

"After My Second Hurricane" published in *Falling Star Magazine* (Spring 2012)

"File Footage" published in *Straight Forward Poetry* (2012)

"Her Mouth" published in *OVS Magazine* (Winter 2013) and reprinted in *The Binnacle* (Spring 2013)

"Full of Grace" published in *The Binnacle* (Spring 2013)

"Nostalgic Scroll" published in *The Way the Light Slants*, Silly Tree Anthologies (2014)

"Hung-Over" published in *Puff Puff Prose Poetry and a Play* (2014)

"Exercising Again" published in *ETA Journal* (2014)

"Great Grandmother Maude's Funeral" published

in *The Way the Light Slants,* Silly Tree Anthologies (2014)

"Dig" published in *Writers Tribe Review* (2015)

"Most Nights" published in *Amore: Love Poems,* Imagination Press (2016)

"Misbehaving" published in *Number One: A Literary Journal* (2017)

"The Price is Right" published in *Number One: A Literary Journal* (2017)

"Smoke Break" published in *Jokes Review* (2017)

"Walk" forthcoming in *A Walk with Nature: Poetic Encounters that Nourish the Soul* (2019)

Praise for Call My Name

"and give them / no chance to ignore me." The power and danger of seeing and being seen is at the core of *Call My Name*. The title of the collection is both a tender prayer and an unflinching demand. In *Call My Name*, Heather Wyatt shows herself as a lyric poet daring enough to show her true faces to the world—faces that reflect wonder and humor and joy and anger and loss. But more than anything, these faces serve as proof of the poet's willingness to bare herself to the world and dare her world to do the same.

—Jason McCall, author of *Silver,*
I Can Explain, and *Dear Hero*

Heather Wyatt's poems take a second look at things, as if she were re-evaluating her experience. With humor and precision, whether she is exploring childhood memories or re-imagining a recent walk with her dog, she gives us the real details, the key images that resonate.

—Greg Pape, author of *Four Swans*
Montana Poet Laureate, emeritus

These poems explore the boundaries and infinite potential of the mundane world. The same bodily reflexes that betray vanity, lust, and shame become the gateways to the spirit and the connective tissue that binds us to others, and even to ourselves. Wyatt conjures snapshots from memory that prove that we see ourselves best through the mirrors others provide us; and that we learn by seeing and continually re-seeing those images.

[. . .]

We are reminded that our identities are dynamic, never static, and that revisitation can be an act of intimacy, forgiveness, and deep friendship to the self. This beautiful work invites us into the mysteries and paradoxes of our humanity with humor, candor and deep vision.

—Ashley McWaters, author of Whitework

ABOUT THE AUTHOR

Heather Wyatt is a teacher and writer by day and food TV junkie by night. Her first book, *My Life Without Ranch* from 50/50 Press features that love of food, but also explores the dangerous relationship we can all have with it. She lives in Tuscaloosa, Alabama and has a slight obsession with her two dogs. She both graduated from and instructs English at the University of Alabama.

She received her MFA from Spalding University in Louisville, Kentucky in poetry. Several of her poems have been featured in a number of journals including *Number One, Puff Puff Prose Poetry and a Play, The Binnacle, ETA, Writers Tribe Review* and many others. Her short story "A Penny Saved" was published in *Perspectives Magazine* in 2018. Her essay "Self-Defense" is in *The Doctor T.J. Eckleburg Review*, September 2018 and her essay, "Hot AF" is in the magazine *Robot Butt*.

Follow her on Twitter @heathermwyatt or visit her website at heathermwyatt.com for more information.

ABOUT THE POETRY BOX

The Poetry Box was founded by Shawn Aveningo Sanders & Robert Sanders, who wholeheartedly believe that every day spent with the people you love, doing what you love, is a moment in life worth cherishing. Their boutique press celebrates the talents of their fellow artisans and writers through professional book design and publishing of individual collections, as well as their flagship literary journal, *The Poeming Pigeon*.

Feel free to visit the online bookstore (thePoetryBox.com), where you'll find more titles including:

Broadfork Farm by Tricia Knoll

November Quilt by Penelope Scambly Schott

Shrinking Bones by Judy K. Mosher

Epicurean Ecstasy by Cynthia Gallaher

The Poet's Curse by Michael Estabrook

Surreal Expulsion by D.R. James

The Unknowable Mystery of Other People by Sally Zakariya

Impossible Ledges by Dianne Avey

Bee Dance by Cathy Cain

and more . . .